THE FARM BOOK

WRITTEN AND ILLUSTRATED BY JAN PFLOOG

A GOLDEN BOOK • NEW YORK
Western Publishing Company, Inc., Racine, Wisconsin 53404

Copyright © 1964 Western Publishing Company, Inc. All rights reserved. Printed in the U.S.A. No part of this book may be reproduced or copied in any form without written permission from the publisher. GOLDEN®, GOLDEN & DESIGN®, A GOLDEN SUPER SHAPE BOOK®, and A GOLDEN BOOK® are trademarks of Western Publishing Company, Inc. ISBN: 0-307-58117-9 ISBN: 0-307-68905-0 (lib. bdg.)
MCMXCIII

Early in the morning
the farmer feeds and milks his cows.

He gives hay to the sheep.
Betty hugs the wooly lambs.

She gives sugar to the ponies.
Her father gives them hay and oats.

Next he feeds the greedy pigs.

Bobby does morning chores, too.
He gives his calf a breakfast of skim milk.

The hungry chickens want their food.
Percival the pet pig wants some, too.

When all the animals are fed,
it is time to go to school.

Hurry, don't miss the bus!

Today the farmer is plowing. Soon he will plant seeds in the softened earth.

After school the children like to go with their father to feed the turkeys.

Best of all, they like to ride their ponies.

It is fun to go to the duck pond.
The ducks are glad Betty has brought corn.

Betty and Bobby are glad that Mother has fried chicken for supper!